Secrets From the Middle:
Making Who You Are Work For You

Elyse S. Scott

Association for Middle Level Education
Westerville, Ohio

Printed in the United States of America.

Library of Congress Cataloging-in-Publication Data

Scott, Elyse S.
  Secrets from the middle: making who you are work for you / Elyse S. Scott.
     pages cm
  ISBN 978-1-56090-254-6
  1. Middle school education. 2. Middle school students. 3. Middle school teaching.
  I. Title.
  LB1623.S396 2013
  373.236--dc23
                              2013027260

Dedication

_____

For Alice, who always said I was a natural born teacher.

For my husband, Allan, who gave me the space and support I relied upon.

For my daughter Kelly and the grandgirls, who gave me my humanity

and

For all my middle school students, who allowed me to discover and be who I am.

About the Author

Elyse S. Scott is a retired English teacher who began her career teaching at the community college level but found her true passion: teaching middle school. With over thirty years of experience teaching at the middle level, she served as mentor for new teachers and cooperating teacher for many student teachers. Her years as an eighth grade team leader gave her invaluable insights into the realities of the multi-dimensional experience unique to middle level education. With wit and wisdom, she writes about what she learned as her career progressed and through decades of guiding teachers through their sometimes overwhelming challenges in the middle. She now writes and consults in the Hudson Valley of New York and is about to see her granddaughter begin her own journey in the middle.

Table of Contents

Author's Note

What I have learned in my almost 30 years of teaching adolescents is that the underlying philosophy driving all other decisions in the classroom has to be: if you can't **reach** them, then you can't **teach** them. Adolescents truly are a strange bunch. You must approach them with an arsenal of tactics that would make a four-star general proud. They need every ounce of compassion, sympathy, empathy, tolerance, humor, and love that you can muster. At the same time, they will draw upon your "inner drill sergeant" as they require strict guidelines, constant repetition of expectations and rules, tough love, and honesty. Above all, they require an infinite amount of patience, patience, and more patience.

If you have come to this book searching for teaching strategies and cool lessons to reel in the adolescents who have their minds set on snagging the cutest boy or the hottest chick or their hearts invested in the latest middle school drama, you really have come to the wrong place. You can find many excellent books chock-full of the latest techniques from do-nows to exit passes, from SQ3Rs to K-W-Ls. Other books will offer suggestions on tapping into students' learning modalities or the domains of Bloom's Taxonomy. These are all noble pursuits in setting up a curriculum, refining instructional strategies, or fostering reading, writing, and critical thinking in any content area.

What you will find on these pages are the fruits of my experiences teaching eighth graders over the past thirty years. Trial and error, many mistakes, tears, and sleepless nights led to my success as a respected teacher in my district. I have found that teaching adolescents is an art form, a craft requiring the honing and sharpening of your skills. Sometimes I liken it to playing golf. The curriculum guides, the instructional materials, the course outlines are the tools of the trade just like a good set of golf clubs. Our professional development opportunities are akin to the golf lessons and tips golfers look for from a pro. But once the fundamentals are addressed, golfers tend to do what comes naturally to them. They add idiosyncratic style to the game, flourishes all their own. If you watch professional golfers, or even those out on the local course, they often have unique ways of addressing the ball, swings that may work for them but would be unorthodox for others, and putting techniques that are far from the norm. Check out their clothing and the way they carry themselves on the course—very individualistic. This is what good middle school teachers do: they invent an approach, a style, and add those flourishes to the good, sound basics of the content of their subject area. They reflect, they agonize, and they go back to the drawing board because that is what good teachers do.

Perhaps you will find among these pages a thing or two or three that you can connect with; may it help you on your own journey through the middle.

Introduction

As with so many teachers, early on, my favorite activity was to play school with my two younger sisters acting as my reluctant but compliant students. It was one thing to play teacher and then decide to be one, but I had many hurdles to cross. I would be the first person in my family to go to college, there were few funds for such an endeavor, and I got little to no advice except the minimal from my high school guidance counselor. With the help of scholarships, my mother's ingenuity, and my own "never let Mom down" guilt complex, I made it through college.

Eventually, I had settled on an English major and am almost embarrassed to say how I arrived at my choice of certification in secondary education, grades 7–12. My age at the time is my only defense—what does a 19-year-old really know about forecasting her life's work? I felt I could not be an elementary school teacher because teaching young children to read was too overwhelming a task and what if I failed them? I also felt this age group was too needy, having had a hand in raising my sisters because my mother worked two jobs and was rarely home. At the high school level, I would have to worry about the New York State English Regents. The strongest argument in my mind was that there was "least harm" in junior high (middle school would be a later concept). In addition, I had what was a most painful adolescence, rife with out-of-whack hormones, an alcoholic father, and a textbook case of low self-esteem. I thought I would, at least, be an empathetic teacher who had walked in my students' shoes.

Who knew that when I was ready to face the job market, I'd be grateful for any job? In the early 70s, tons of students were looking for scant jobs, and I would have to teach part time at the local community college for quite a few years before making my way into a public school position. But the gods were with me, and finally I landed a position teaching grades 7 and 8, and I taught at that school for the rest of my career. Like all those teaching in middle school, I came to realize that we are kind of the black hole in between elementary school and high school. Our "clients" don't necessarily put education as a high priority on their list. They have too many other things they are dealing with, some completely out of their control. I would always marvel at year's end of eighth grade how incredibly different our students would look in June compared to their yearbook picture that had been taken sometime in October or early November! Imagine what was going on inside of those children's minds and bodies.

If you ask middle school students their number one reason for coming to school, they will usually say it is to see their friends. That is pretty stiff competition for teachers. In elementary school most students are still in awe of the process: it is the age of discovery for them, and they want to please their teachers. By high school most students have to get serious about the not-so-distant future of a job or college; for many it is a settling down time. But the middle is exactly that: a transition time when students are bridging the gap between childhood and maturity. Adolescents are known to cross that bridge many times in a single day!

All of this being said, what is our goal after all? It is to have our students learn and learn deeply. We want them to internalize what we have taught them and learn valuable life lessons along the way. The secret to accomplishing this was to reach my students, truly get inside their minds and hearts. In order to do that, I had to exert Herculean efforts all day, every day.

1

Know Yourself

Okay, so it doesn't matter how you ended up in a middle school or junior high. Perhaps it has always been your aspiration to teach at this level. More commonly these days, that's where the job offer was, and beggars cannot be choosers in this climate. Or perhaps, even more difficult for some, you were transferred from high school, and this is awakening a whole other teaching zone in your brain! While I don't want to talk anyone down from the high of landing a job, I must caution against idealism and unrealistic dreams. The best way to enter a middle school is with "eyes wide open" and with extreme caution. Perhaps at your interview, with a certain detached perspective, you noted the high energy and bubbling enthusiasm of the hallways reaching an almost chaotic pitch. In reality, the atmosphere in a middle school can be quiet and laid-back some days and at a feverish pitch on others. The middle school can seem like a laboratory for hands-on, inquiry-based learning on its best days, and, quite frankly, a cuckoo's nest on others. Most times it is somewhere in between. If you know that going in, you learn to adjust your internal barometer to what is normal.

Analyze your tolerance level.
It helps to analyze your tolerance level for this "new normal," as I call it. I have had many colleagues who operate very well in an atmosphere of organized chaos. They thrive on the high energy, the feverish pitch. I never was one of them, even at the beginning of my career, so it has nothing to do with increasing age or crankiness. I always needed an organized, calm atmosphere in which I could thrive, and I knew early on I couldn't teach

students if I wasn't in a comfortable place for me. Adolescents will take their cues from you. You don't have to be dogmatic or unreasonable. I have found that if you explain who you are as a person and why you do the things you do, kids are willing to listen. So, decide where you fit in the scheme of things. Envision what your classroom will look like, how it will "run" for forty-five minutes or so, and how your students will act in that room. Having a clear vision with eyes wide open allows you to lay out a blueprint for your role, your students' role, and the logistics of your classroom. You don't want to do this after the fact; it is so difficult in middle school to undo what is already done!

> **Lay out a blueprint for your role, your students' role, and the logistics of your classroom.**

Embrace flexibility and choice.

After many years of establishing routines that worked and tweaking things that did not, I offer this advice. Workshops on classroom organization, behavior management, and lesson design are incredibly helpful. But the real beauty of professional development was its offering of a menu from which I was free to choose what appealed to me within the vision I had for my own classroom. In working with younger teachers, I found that they often feel they have to take what they have learned as gospel with no room for flexibility and choice. Your classroom must be your creation, not some "should be" model offered up by well-meaning colleagues, education websites, or textbooks. I always told my students that my classroom was my home away from home, and I fostered an atmosphere that was calming, welcoming, and interesting with plenty of room for active engagement in the lessons. There are plenty of successful teachers who run on high gear, but I have usually found that at the center of it all is a modicum of structure and clear guidelines.

> **The real beauty of professional development was its offering of a menu from which I was free to choose.**

Make *who you are* work for you.

The same holds true for your vision of yourself as "teacher." You are who you are. You have a personality, a background, a belief system. To survive in a classroom with adolescents, you cannot turn on or off who you really are. That would be incredibly exhausting. Of course, you can make modifications and adjustments—that is called survival. The key is to make "who you are" work for you and ultimately for your students. Another way of looking at it is this: How would you want the curriculum you must deliver imparted to you if you were on the receiving end? What would make you listen and take notice? What kind of person do you trust, respect, and look up to?

> **To survive in a classroom with adolescents, you cannot turn on or off who you really are.**

Therein lies the secret of the whole experience. What can you give as a unique human being that will first establish trust? What can only **you** give as a human being that will yield respect? What can only **you** give as a human being that will keep them coming back interested and enthusiastic? Notice I used the word *give* not *do*. Secret Number One: You must be a giving human being first; a teacher, second.

2

Authenticity and Trust

Trust by its very definition is established over time, and teachers only have a finite amount of time to build this essential ingredient. In order to make connections with students, prompt them to be explorers and discoverers, and ask them to take risks and go beyond their comfort levels, teachers must gain their trust. However, you don't just walk into a classroom and trust happens. Adolescents are skeptical and suspicious; they pride themselves on their ability to spot a phony and loathe hypocrisy. Actually, they have a sixth sense about it. So yet again, the middle school teacher has a Herculean task: establish trust, the key ingredient in the student/teacher relationship; do it quickly; and have it inform all of one's thoughts, deeds, and actions. The key question is: What must I do to earn students' trust?

> **The key question is: What must I do to earn students' trust?**

Elements of trust.

In examining the trust factor in all my relationships, I find some commonalities. I trust my husband because I can count on him to follow through on his promises; if he says he is going to do something, I know it will happen. That is true of all those who are truly close to me. I trust my doctor because he listens to me, cares about me as a person first; patient, second; he is knowledgeable in his field, yet he explains himself in terms I can understand. The friends that I trust the most are the people in my life who accept me for who I am, appreciate my gifts and talents, and are always there when I need them most. I even trust salesmen when they lose the veneer, talk to me person-to-person, and are genuine and sincere. These people are honest and have integrity; they listen with intensity; they are dependable and responsible; and they easily translate their brand of intelligence.

Students who earned my trust could be counted on: they followed through on assignments and met deadlines and other school obligations. Hard workers, they consistently put forth their best efforts. They were leaders because they were good listeners, cooperative, and empathetic. Most of all, although they may not have been A+ students, they had practical wisdom and knew how to access information they needed. If I expected those qualities from my students in order to trust them, then I had to be someone they could count on to keep promises, listen with full attention, be accountable at all times, and not only be on top of my game about my subject matter, but impart my wisdom and insights about life.

The greatest element of trust.
However, I think the greatest factor that led to gaining the trust of my students was to present my authentic self to them. I had learned very early on that honesty and self-revelation have their own kind of power. As the child of an alcoholic living in a household that was extremely dysfunctional, I was the classic introvert and lived with shame and a certain envy of others whose lives seemed so well-adjusted and normal. I took a chance on my college application essay and wrote about how that childhood had affected me and what I hoped this new phase in my life would afford me. In fact, when I began my student teaching, my supervisor told me that when she had read that essay, she was very moved by it and knew that I had life experience that would be an asset in dealing with children. From then on I was much less guarded about where I came from, and while I certainly did not wear my troubled background as a "badge of honor," I would come to accept that it was a part of me just like any other facet of my being.

> **Honesty and self-revelation have their own kind of power.**

In the early years of my career, I did not discuss my personal background except with the occasional struggling student whose background was similar to mine. However, as I became more confident in the classroom, I shared some of my childhood experiences as natural extensions of what we were reading or discussing. Young adult literature is replete with misfits with whom I easily identified, so I was able to discuss my childhood issues in the context of literature. And through the years, as more and more students came into my teaching life from broken homes due to divorce, alcohol, drugs, or a combination of these factors, it became much more natural to discuss my childhood and how I managed to overcome so many of the obstacles that might have seemed insurmountable to my students who were living with dysfunction at that time.

Using authenticity to connect with students.

Revealing my true self did not diminish my worth in my students' eyes; in fact, my sharing increased it. It was simply another way I could connect with adolescents. Later on when I supervised many student teachers, the trust component was always a hot topic of discussion. In some cases former students of my English class became my student teachers; imagine the kind of feedback that provided! As young adults they could remember the "humanity" of my class in addition to the academics, the choice of writing topics and reading selections that required their unique personal perspective based on their own experiences, and

> **Revealing my true self did not diminish my worth in my students' eyes; in fact, my sharing increased it.**

the modeling I had done for them in talking about difficult experiences in my life so that they could feel comfortable doing the same in an environment of trust. I gave all my student teachers an actual assignment before they began their practicum with me: to think of ways they could reveal their authentic selves and make connections to my students from the very first day in my classroom. That was the only successful way to make that required shift from Mrs. Scott to new-teacher-in charge. And there was no sitting in the back of the room those first few weeks, because in that scenario, there are no trust-building possibilities. I did, however, have my student teachers react to student writing in which they made their first contacts with each student, one-on-one. Student teachers helped students with their work, sat in during group work, and hung out in the cafeteria during the students' lunch periods. Having free reign to develop a mini-unit reflecting their expertise and passion, they learned to reveal "who they really were" and gained the trust of students. Trust breeds trust, and students were supportive of the student teachers rather than wishing them gone! The secret to trust building is like any other teaching skill: it develops not only with the experience of working with students but also by getting to know who you are in the classroom and gaining trust in yourself.

Trust develops by getting to know who you are in the classroom, gaining trust in yourself, and working with students.

3

Getting to Know You

When you take the helm in a middle school classroom, first impressions count just as they do in any other aspect of your life. But expect adolescents to keep you at arm's length for a while. Adolescents, though often all bravado and together on the outside, have a bit of the "frightened puppy syndrome" lurking inside. If you've ever watched a new pup's encounter with a stranger, often the pup takes two steps back for every advance, a sort of sniffing the stranger out then backing away, maybe lingering awhile for a time, then retreating. The process of establishing a relationship with a middle school teacher is gradual for most students, and ironically, I have found that the students who seemed aloof or suspicious at first were the very ones with whom I built an amazing student/teacher bond.

> **The process of establishing a relationship with a middle school teacher is gradual for most students.**

As an academic under pressure about standards and testing, you may be inclined to begin delivering your curriculum when the school year begins. My advice is to present yourself as a human being first. Reflect a bit and focus on your personal priorities for teaching.

- What brings you to stand before these children?

- What do you think they should know about you before you begin the academic journey?

- Can you translate your vision into words that will get them hooked into you first and then into where you want to take them?

- If you have your own classroom, does the environment have your "signature" on it?

Focus on your personal priorities for teaching. Far from being an aside, an extra, something that matters less than the academic goals you have for your students, knowing and focusing on these issues will be the foundation upon which all your middle school students' success is built.

Creatively start the year.

How you start the year off—or begin a leave replacement or whatever your circumstances might be—paves the way for all that will follow. Tap into your creativity on this one. Is there a talent you have or cool idea that will give your students pause, rather than repeat what they may have already heard myriad periods in a row? As an English teacher, I discovered my inner poet early on, and so I introduced myself, the rules for my classroom, my expectations, and my likes and dislikes via a rhyming poem. Kids thought that was way cool, but believe me, I got my points across! What are you passionate about that you can start building relationships with students on? Even if they don't share the exact same passion, they will recognize and identify with the surge of energy and enthusiasm you have for it because they have such interests of their own. It gives them something to start asking questions about (So, a poem can have RULES in it?), make snap judgments about (But, you're a TEACHER; you CAN'T ride your bike to school!) and realize that the world is broader and more interesting than they previously imagined.

Set limits.

Never be afraid to establish firm guidelines in *your* classroom. One of the secrets of working with adolescents is to embrace the fact that this age group craves limitations. They will question them, they will test them, but they feel better knowing that you are in control. Because I explained why I expected certain behaviors and we would follow routines in particular situations, I rarely had classroom management issues. Rather than long harangues or "because I said so" speeches, I often said things like, "How would you like it if....." in the case of touching my things; or I told them a quick story about "What could happen if....." when it regarded their safety. And because all my students had pet peeves and could totally relate, explaining mine as they pertained to my classroom made sense to them.

Define your role.

Early on in my work with teens, I realized that I had to define my role. I was never their friend. Mentor, check. Facilitator of learning, check. However, I was never "one of them," and at times I had to remind my students of that fact. Middle school students need periodic reminders about boundaries, tone of voice, and expectations. Especially very young, new teachers (and I have talked to many) must draw a line in the

I was never their friend.

sand and strike a balance between being "with it" and "the adult in charge." It's easy and tempting to fall into a trap by thinking, "I can so relate to these kids; it wasn't so long ago that I was in their shoes." It's great to be cool, but not *too* cool.

Most teachers learn soon enough that their role in their students' lives encompasses much more than delivering curriculum. Nowhere is it more apparent that a teacher wears many different hats than at the middle level; teachers must be ready to play the sub-roles of parent, school specialist, guidance counselor/social worker, referee, fashion advisor, spiritual leader, and salesperson. In fact, you will often hear a middle school teacher declare, "I never have enough time to teach my subject!"

Parental sub-role.

Perhaps, the most obvious sub-role for a middle school teacher is that of parent, or for younger teachers, confidante. Of course, all teachers wear this parent hat, especially the elementary school nurturer, but when donning the hat of surrogate parent in my middle school classroom, I played the part of stern mother with lectures from 1 to 502! I usually delivered them with yardstick in hand, and my students knew they were in for some motherly advice or lessons on etiquette and manners. Sometimes adolescents forget where they are or were never taught a bit of decorum, so I would stop when necessary and, though chuckling on the inside, get very serious and show them the light. Adolescents are renowned for sharpening a pencil when none is needed or passing gas for just the right spark of entertainment when important life questions are explored during in-depth discussions. I cannot tell you how many times my classes would be involved in a story, and students would raise their hands and ask questions out of the blue like, "Did you dye your hair?" or "Is that watch new?" or "Do you know what's for lunch today?" I think I have a hundred variations on the eye roll in my repertoire!

Many times students sought me out for advice in lieu of their own parents— probably as a safer testing ground. Typical topics in middle school: peer pressure, concerns about grades or a particular teacher, worries about the poor health of a family member, sibling issues, getting a job, family money issues. Typically, if there is a societal woe, it will find its way into a middle school classroom. In addition, middle school drama can present itself in a nanosecond, and I always had to be at the ready with good, sound advice, often relying on my own mothering of a teen back in the day.

School specialist sub-role.
Often you wear all the different school specialist hats in one class period. This allows you to avoid the alternative of sending students out to see various specialists which is time-consuming, involves a pass, and results in students missing class time in transit to these various venues. For example, if given half a chance, most adolescents could easily spend half their school day in the nurse's office. It's a change of environment, seeing a different face, and maybe doing some socializing going to and fro. Of course, there are certain "no brainers" such as when students are truly ill; in these cases, I insisted that they make a beeline for the nurse's office, pass or no pass. However, in the gray areas, differential diagnosis is required, and usually it's attention or peace of mind a student is looking for. I always kept band aids, sanitizer, and wipes in my classroom because those would be the top three reasons to head to the nurse.

Guidance counselor/social worker.

I also played guidance counselor and social worker almost every day. Adolescents have a burning need to tell all and crave a supportive audience. Again, with experience, you become a good judge of what constitutes a need for immediate counseling with the experts, but teachers can usually handle the broken heart department, best friend dilemmas, and the rumor mill. When students would come in with tears in their eyes, sometimes a warm, "Are you okay?" would take care of it. Sometimes just a quick conversation would smooth it over so the student could go on with the class. You learn to follow your gut instincts on the Middle School Drama Scale. When in doubt, it's best to let your students get that bit of guidance from someone else.

Referee.

Any good middle school teacher worth his or her salt had better be ready to don the old referee's cap. Adolescents are a contentious bunch: student vs student, student vs teacher, student vs the world. Adolescents also want to be heard: they feel entitled to voice their opinions, even at inopportune times. Be prepared to simultaneously don both the ref's cap and the diplomat's hat because while you are calling the plays as you see them, you also must be mindful of the most important outcome for your student: saving face. For all the clowning, effervescence, or bravado on the surface of most middle school kids, right below the surface is a very fragile, tender heart. The most important responsibility I had, contrary to what the standards writers and the Ed Department test bureau had in mind, was to tend to the vulnerable psyches of my middle school students!

> **You must be mindful of the most important outcome for your student: saving face.**

Fashion advisor.

From ref to fashion advisor! How do you make that leap? Now, one would think this would be totally out of our realm as teachers, but students look to the adults in the building for affirmation. Most times it was very easy to compliment student attempts at being fashionistas. As I stood outside my door between classes, students would ask me to check them out. "Do you like my new outfit?" "What do you think of my piercing?" "Aren't these Uggs cool with these short shorts?" "What do you think of my green/purple hair?" As fashion advisor/diplomat, I was dealing with delicate egos. Noncommittal responses might be in order, something like, "What matters most is what you think...." Unless you have a good, specific student dress code, then perhaps, the time it takes to fill out a pass to the office might be worth it. I'm thinking of revealing tops; short, short shorts; skimpy items—you just might not want to go there.

Role model.

No, you didn't ask to be anyone's role model, but the students feel you should be. Although they know *they* are not perfect and they know *they* are allowed to make mistakes, most students expect *you* to be perfect. They are profoundly shocked and distressed by your slip of the tongue or your less-than-perfect response to a question. You must face the fact that you have a captive audience in front of you each and every day. Students know every subtlety of your mannerisms, your speech patterns, your fashion sense or lack thereof, seemingly everything! Bad word? Bad joke? Bad hair day? Bad outfit day? You'll hear about it. I remember my own daughter coming home from middle school. When I would ask, "What's new at school?" she could never remember one academic piece of information, but could do a first-rate impression of each and every one of her teachers. The secret with my students was to own up, tongue-in-cheek, of course, "I never said I was perfect" or "I'll try harder next time."

> Students know every subtlety of your mannerisms, your speech patterns, and your fashion sense or lack thereof.

Spiritual leader sub-role.

Although you may not choose to wear this hat, you may find yourself in the role of theologian, or for the non-denominational, spiritual leader. In the throes of defining who they are, making sense of the world in which they live, and seeking answers about universal truths, adolescents dwell on death and the mystery behind it. While I never proselytized or spouted my views, I could never refuse to discuss their questions, and my teaching of English gave me a wide berth to discuss some of life's big questions. However, if students' ponderings made me truly uncomfortable, I told them so in a kind, nonthreatening way. I would suggest that perhaps these topics were better discussed at home. When I would say, "Moving right along..." they came to understand my drift.

Salesperson sub-role.

Shifting gears now, one of the most interesting hats I often wore was my salesperson's hat. Middle school students basically look for entertainment in a classroom, their favorite word being "fun." While I was fortunate to have the variety a language arts curriculum provides, middle school students were increasingly skeptical about reading and writing. When I assigned a novel, they would typically ask, "How long is it?" or "How big is the print?" or "Can we have a long time to read it?" Even the great classics of adolescent fiction like S.E. Hinton's *The Outsiders* or Paul Zindel's *The Pigman* required selling.

And writing??!! My selling point was that no matter what career path they might take in the future, they would have to be able to write competently. And those were the easy sales! Making grammar, research, and public speaking palatable, I appealed to middle school students' concern about appearance and how they are perceived—that those skills were a reflection on them and spoke volumes to others. I connected the skills to real-world job interviews, applying to colleges, and pursuing volunteer and other activities. Sharing very poorly written letters-to-the-editor from the local newspaper in terms of grammar, use of language, and lack of substance supported my sales pitch every time.

Decline without judgment.

That brings me to a general point about any hat you are asked to wear in teaching, any role that you are assigned. You can always decline. That goes for absolutely anything, within reason of course, that goes against your grain in any given school day. I think the secret, though, in dealing with adolescents is that there is a right way to do it. No matter what bothers you, you can be nonjudgmental, laid-back, and definitely nonthreatening. I always relied on the old adage, "It's not what you say, but how you say it." I think that's what always mattered most to my students. I tried to be cool, calm, and calculated in my dealings with my students, especially in the tough spots. I know I always felt better in the end when I hadn't resorted to sarcasm or put downs. Trust me, I needed to be sleeping, not tossing, turning, and ruminating about something I had said, so I could be at my best to face yet another day of wearing all those hats.

The secret to a successful beginning is to start off with real conviction about your expectations, firmness in establishing guidelines, clarity in your role; then creativity, humor, and compassion go a long way in softening the edges of that first impression. I noticed over the years that "the skittish puppy syndrome" lasted about a month, but would always be replaced by trust, respect, and a playing field where we all knew our positions.

4

To Be or Not To Be Popular

By most people's standards of popularity, I qualified as a "popular" teacher in my school district. Parents requested me and my name was a known quantity among students progressing to the eighth grade. I say this not with arrogance but to prove a point about what "popularity" can mean. Never once did I throw a party in my class (well, maybe a couple for very special occasions, but I gave a lecture on crumbs!), give out rewards in the form of candy or cookies, or run Friday films (well, maybe if a planned film worked into that day). I did not give "no homework nights" or drop the lowest grade. Now a system of rewards, whether candy, cookies, redeemable tickets, or gifts, works for some teachers. My only caveat is that such a system may have unintended consequences. First, adolescents often want bigger and better rewards when enthusiasm over the originals wanes. Second, there can be a negative domino effect when lollipop sucking, gum chewing students take the fruits of their rewards to other classrooms where they are not welcome. Third, it can be downright messy. Your best friends in any school happen to be the custodians (another secret, by the way), and you want them on your side. Crumbs, candy papers, and wads of gum translate to extra work for them. As my career progressed and I became increasingly concerned about the number of students coping with food allergies, I really did not want food of any kind in my classroom. My students totally understood my logical explanation without delving into the potential distraction from learning that sugar highs and lows would have added.

My brand of popularity was articulated when I retired. Synonyms for my particular appeal were "committed to children," "dedicated," "passionate," "hardworking," and "respected." Again, the secret to connecting with adolescents comes back to your own vision of what your role of teacher is. I learned early on that my own background as a student and my principles and ethics would be the guiding forces in all that I did as a teacher.

What worked for you as a middle school student?

When I started my education courses in college and eventually did my student teaching, I instinctively looked back to my own junior high years, just as new parents look back to how they were parented. I can't say I was brimming with happiness or nostalgia for what really were not "the good old days" for me. While I was a good student, did my work religiously, and was well-mannered and behaved, I was a hormonal, insecure, down-in-the dumps young lady. There were many things about my junior high school education that would come to inform the way I did things in my own classroom. I felt teachers had their classic "pets"—I tried never to have them or, at least, never make it known. Many teachers simply lectured, and we took notes. Even before experiencing all the cool, creative professional development workshops and in-services, I knew that I had to engage students by making every lesson I taught meaningful and relevant to their lives somehow. As a student I remember waiting weeks to get tests and papers back. I made and followed through on a vow to get all paperwork back to my students in a timely fashion. I often felt that classrooms were dull, lifeless places, and so my rooms through the years reflected my home away from home: warm, welcoming, displaying interesting posters, student art, and framed student writing. Students noticed, believe me. I often discussed my own adolescent years with the students themselves, and in doing so, I may have erased many of their same doubts, insecurities, and issues.

> I often discussed my own adolescent years with the students, and in doing so, I may have erased many of their same doubts, insecurities, and issues.

Tell students why you believe in your principles.

I rarely backed off from my guiding principles through the years, and I let students know why I believed in them. For example, while a colleague next door might let them do certain things against school rules, they had to understand it was my job to enforce school rules—like them or not. Inconsistency is rife in middle school, and while I would never talk about other teachers, I would hold the party line on "this is what I do in my classroom."

It is a middle schooler's nature to call out, butt into a heated discussion, or to dismiss another's opinion as "stupid" or tell someone to "shut up." Those were strict "no-nos" in my room. But instead of simply posting rules about raising hands or showing respect, I was passionate about explaining the "whys" behind them. No student ever argued with my philosophy that fear could not be part of the landscape in my classroom; that every student had a right to say what he or she believed without repercussion; and that I would have had my mouth washed out with soap for saying "stupid" or "shut up" to my sisters, so the words were particularly offensive to me. Also, I didn't simply say all this; I led by example.

> I never apologized for assigning reading and writing but spoke passionately and without compromise about these endeavors as the key to all learning!

When it came to the work I assigned, I would make the assignments meaningful, tap into their creativity, and most importantly, stimulate their thinking, not provide busy work. However, I never apologized for assigning reading and writing but spoke passionately and without compromise about these endeavors as the key to all learning!

Admit mistakes.

I always tried to do the right thing by my students. If I was wrong, I admitted it. I apologized. If I messed up, I let them know it. Students can be so forgiving if their teacher is not defensive or in denial. I was honest when I could be about school and office procedures—why we did them, their purpose. I think students knew they would get a straight answer from me. But I was also honest enough to tell them that though surely I would keep their confidences (I was no Svengali)—some things had to be shared with guidance counselors and principals for their own safety and well-being.

> Students can be so forgiving if their teacher is not defensive or in denial.

I was always cognizant of the line between student and teacher and painful judgment calls, but I laid it all out in the early days of each school year.

Find ways to validate them.

As I grew in my profession, I had one of those "ah-hah" moments that became the one, clear driving force in my dealings with my students. It was so simple really—the old "golden rule"—if you will. "Treat others as you would have them......." You know the drill. If you want to put it into more philosophical terms: I reduced my classroom practice to what I believe is the common denominator for all human beings—the need to be validated. That became my goal each year with every new batch of students: finding ways to validate each one, celebrating their gifts, redeeming even the most abrasive, irksome "hooligans", as I called them, who crossed my threshold.

> I reduced my classroom practice to what I believe is the common denominator for all human beings—the need to be validated.

Never in my career did I try to be popular. My secret was to build a career on a foundation of all the intrinsic factors that motivated me as a human being and an increasing understanding of what adolescents really needed— firmness, honesty, and respect. I also opened doors and pathways so that my students could discover their own self-worth. And isn't that what we all crave in our lives?

5

Be Irresistible

So if teaching in middle school is not about popularity, what is it that makes students what I call "pickers and choosers"? They go into one room and are well-behaved and on target; in other rooms a whole negative side of their personality will manifest itself. You will hear teachers say, "Oh! He's great for me!" while another teacher wrings her hands over what she sees as her failure with this student. In one word, teachers must be "irresistible." But what makes it so intriguing is that "irresistible" can have so many definitions and descriptions, an elixir that draws students into their teachers' worlds. It is not formulaic; in fact, having supervised many student teachers over the course of my career, it was the one aspect of their development that I had much

> **Teachers have to find that personality trait, or talent, or background experience that sets them apart and draws students to them like a magnet.**

difficulty nurturing. Teachers have to find that personality trait, or talent, or background experience that sets them apart and draws students to them like a magnet. Once students are hooked, teachers have to find ways to be irresistible all the time. Okay, that would mean they are superhuman. Be irresistible *most* of the time.

Show how you've dealt with adversity.
My secret with middle school students was making connections in many different ways. For some students, the connection was that I had a painful adolescence. So many could relate to the experiences I shared with them. Many of my students came from torn, dysfunctional families. Sharing early

on what it was like to live with an alcoholic father and how lack of money was always an issue resonated with many of them. I was quick to point out, however, that I never used it as an excuse to check out from my responsibilities, and they could see in the living flesh a survivor, someone who had worked hard and gone on to higher education, got a job, had a family, and was standing before them as their teacher. Some students thought it cool that I am a golfer and loved to discuss their game with me. Others were enthralled with my tales of world travel, especially when I could bring to life settings of stories we were reading in class.

> They could see a survivor, someone who had worked hard and gone on to higher education, got a job, had a family, and was standing before them as their teacher.

Capitalize on your flaws.

I even drew many students into my circle by capitalizing on, of all things, my flaws. I would always admit to my students that while I had many talents, art was never one of them. I'd make futile attempts to draw something on the board and they loved coming to my rescue. I'd always point out that we all "win some and lose some" in this life. Over the years as technology progressed and this late learner was often all thumbs, students would help me and rescue me from all kinds of trouble on the computer. All of this served to illustrate that their teacher was human! We shared so many laughs over the years—how irresistible is that!

Share stories to bring insight.

I also told lots of stories to my students. It was easy to inject them into teaching English, but going off on an occasional tangent was good for the students' souls as well as mine and fostered new connections at every turn. I never hesitated to share a story about former students or something that happened with a student I had that particular year. Good stories only, of course, unless I had a student's permission to tell about a learning experience they had or a deep moment of insight they did not mind sharing. When possible, I had the students share with their classmates. I also shared the travails of raising my own daughter, especially tales of her adolescence, and I would watch their eyes roll or heads nod with empathy, sometimes for the mother, their teacher, and sometimes the daughter with whom they could totally commiserate. My students always knew that I had a handle on their out-of-school experiences, their other lives.

Connect with personal notes.

Perhaps, the greatest connections I made, and the ones former students remember most, were through my writing. Now these were the most time-consuming of all my endeavors, but the connections I was able to make with the written word touched thousands of lives over the course of my career. As educators we all know that papers have to be graded, but I learned early on that red correction marks and a grade in the upper right hand corner made very little impact. What my students treasured most were the mini-letters I wrote at the bottom of their work in which I commented on areas in need of improvement, suggestions, and most importantly, what strengths I found, what had touched me—that human voice of validation. I was also known to hand notes written on stationery to students, sometimes

> **Make that one-on-one connection via a note—because sometimes a face-to-face is tough for adolescents.**

to praise them, but especially if I was noting behaviors that I did not want to see turn into full-blown issues. I wish I could tell you how many problems I nipped in the bud because of those notes. Someone, a teacher, had taken the time to make that one-on-one connection via one of the favorite middle school modes of communication—the note—because sometimes a face-to-face is tough for some adolescents.

Work along with students.

My most irresistible attraction was writing along with my students. If I gave an assignment, I did it too. Sometimes I would model for them, but often I sat among them and composed a paragraph, an essay, a poem. I loved these moments because it allowed me the forum to explain that I did not always consider myself a writer, but through time, practice, and reflection, I uncovered a bit of writing talent, and I'd see it happen over and over again for many of my students who previously believed they couldn't write.

In fact, I loved to sit at a student desk whenever the chance arose: during student presentations, watching a film, or monitoring student discussions. I actually spent very little time at my desk when kids were present, and I think that registered with them.

Find ways to compliment them.

Adolescents are often so down on themselves or into the drama du jour that they seem surprised at the power of a kind word or two. Never falsely, but from the heart, I would try to find ways to compliment my students, welcome them back from an absence, or ask how older siblings I once had were doing. As teachers we get so mired in our days that we forget we are dealing with children. Between the issues of our outside world and those within the school community, we get so bogged down sometimes that we forget these simple connections and the power they have.

Leave negative emotions at the door.

Speaking of the outside world, it's difficult to leave all the things that bother us at the school door. However, I learned early on that middle schoolers pick up on their teachers' moods and have even branded some teachers as "too moody." I always tried to leave my emotions at the door, often giving myself pep talks during hall passing time and taking deep breaths before entering. My students would often mention that I was the same Mrs. Scott day in and day out. That took so much work, but I would see the positive benefits in smoother lessons and an upbeat feeling in the room.

No matter what subject you teach, the human dynamic supersedes all in middle school.

Notice that I have not said much about the academic piece. The secret is that no matter what subject you teach, the human dynamic supersedes all in middle school. Successful science labs, art lessons, or math problems are presented by human beings who, hopefully, are "simply irresistible" in their own right.

6

You're On!

I always greeted my students for class just outside my door, and after a hasty response to my "good morning" or "hello," their typical question was, "What are we doing today?" One of my stock answers was, "I should put a marquis outside my door and have 'now playing for your entertainment running across it'.......!!" Then I would tell them they would just have to wait for the surprise.

Truly the word *teacher* is synonymous with *actor*. Certainly part of being an actor in a middle school classroom is playing all the roles I talked about previously. But it is so much more than that. The persona I adopted in my classroom was so different than the real-life person I was and am outside of school. Of course, as the years went on, I would find the dual personalities blending, the lines blurring. I felt that from the time students arrived in the morning until the time I heaved myself into the car each afternoon, the stage light said "ON." What I did each and every day was a performance, with preps and lunch breaks serving as intermissions.

Project energy.
So what constituted these performances? Whether feeling energetic, ebullient, and uplifted or not, I always felt I had to project that image to draw my students in. Of course, there are those doldrums days when you are not feeling well or your personal life is in dire straits, and if you've gained trust and respect from your students and tell them you are having a bad day, they are generally cooperative. But like a sports figure heading out

to the field or a singer about to perform, I would give myself little pep talks and take deep breaths before entering class and closing the door. A dynamic teacher opens the lines of communication, no doubt in my mind.

Rehearse.
But charisma is not enough. Like good actors, I always rehearsed my lines. If I was reading new material to my students, stories or poems, for example, I made sure I read through them with attention to tone, mood, and delivery. Middle school teachers, like actors, must be willing to adapt to any scene. The landscape is ever-changing; the plot is always thickening. Middle school drama is legendary, and you are in the thick of it. You must spontaneously do an impromptu scene brought on by the latest dilemma.

Write a script.
Like good directors, I *always* made a short outline of what I would do in a class period and followed the "script": preparedness is next to godliness when you are dealing with a middle school audience. There can be no holes in the action, and too many dramatic pauses give the class blabbermouth a foot in the door. And like any entertainer, I constantly sought ways to include audience participation whenever possible: "Come on up and show us" or "I need an assistant" were requests I made over and over again. And just as any successful production relies on good planning, I would try never to leave for the day without running through the lineup for the next day, and within reason, I never left unfinished business, so I could start fresh the next day. In middle school new things pop up instantaneously, so unfinished business tends to snowball into next week.

Attention getters.
As technology took its hold on my students over the years, I found that increasing numbers of students had decreasing attention spans. To engage students, I was never above breaking into a song, telling a good joke, or taking a side journey to relate my subject to real life. Since I taught English, I found that props made my stories come alive. I brought out my black plastic rat with red beady eyes for Edgar Allan Poe's "The Pit and the Pendulum" and my stuffed black and white cat for his "The Black Cat." I

displayed my birds for the Daphne DuMaurier story "The Birds" and my mini-pig collection for our reading of *The Pigman*. I had tons of mushy, squishy eyeballs that supported my telling of scary stories. I had a blow-up sword from a Happy Meal that I used to "make my points"! And, of course, there was always my signature yardstick to accompany my "Scott lectures." Middle school students, for all their supposed sophistication, love toys! The greatest blessing of all, though, was that I found my comedic side because you cannot teach middle school if you don't have a sense of humor.

Shtick.

Successful middle school teachers have a common denominator: they all have a shtick. Often, it is not something that can be copied or forced. Middle school teachers have to find that approach that allows them to be a magnet for kids. I learned the most about what middle schoolers need when I had student teachers working with me. I really learned what it means to sit in an uncomfortable chair for forty-five minutes, fidgeting, doodling, and wanting to be part of the action. Through the years I discovered my own shtick was baring my "inner child" to the children I taught: energy, enthusiasm, curiosity, and playfulness. I demanded hard work and excellence but in an environment of inquiry, dialogue, and sheer fun.

> **I demanded hard work and excellence but in an environment of inquiry, dialogue, and sheer fun.**

I researched "their scene" in music, movies, sports, and books, and I shared my findings: what I loved, what I did not love, and what I outright disapproved of and why. I never tried to be one of them, but I did want to know about their world. I love rap music because it is pure poetry, but I could live without the four letter words. I would argue the allure of some of their hot picks for actresses and actors. And I would talk at length about quick rises to fame and the sad consequences sometimes for their "role models." I could talk at length with kids about their world because I made it part of my job description. The acting part always came down to how I dealt with it all—with emotion, with wit, and awareness at all times of who my audience was.

7

It's All in the Details

If middle school teachers were just a tired, haggard, brow-beaten lot, no one would be doing it! Just as in any profession, you have your folks who see it as a job like any other; they are there for the paycheck. But for the most part, middle school teachers are quite an amazing crew.

The common thread.
A diverse bunch, they have varied talents and gifts, they embody a wide range of beliefs and values, and they have emotional ranges from the most serious and somber to the happy-go-lucky, a joke-a-minute types. The common thread among them that weaves the tapestry of middle school life is "being there for kids." Most middle school teachers want to support children during this truly incredible stage of their lives, to assist them in discovery, to excite them about learning, to help them if they are in trouble, and to give them tools for transitioning to high school and then the "real world." They want it so badly they sometimes feel they want it for their students more than the students want it for themselves.

It's that zeal and fervor that drives good middle school teachers. They dig down deep to tap their creativity. They know that extensive preparation yields results. They rarely are happy with the status quo. They are willing to go back to the drawing board and rethink lessons and approaches that may not have been as successful as they had hoped. They are self-reflectors, open to refining their practices. The bottom line is always to get kids excited about learning.

A blank canvas.

If you think about a typical class period, it is like a blank canvas. In order to engage middle school students, a lesson plan is simply not enough. The secret at this level is in the details. A good middle school teacher accounts for almost every minute, start to finish. I had a continuous checklist running through my mind at all times.

- What if a segment finished early; how could I enrich it?

- If I was doing too much talking in one period, how could I draw students in more?

- How could I make sure there was little to no down time?

- Was there a way to extend the lesson to include life experiences and applications?

- Did I have an interesting personal story or film clip to augment what we were learning?

Teacher as facilitator.

As I grew in the teaching profession, I came to think of myself less as "teacher" and more as "facilitator of learning." I started the change slowly. I had students collaborate on the planning of assignments and lessons. When I did that, I noticed that many students seemed to awaken from a previously long sleep! Next, I gave more choice when it came to many assignments; instead of one task, I offered a variety. All of a sudden, students who rarely handed in work, were actually into the assignments. When I moved to more project-based learning, my students were not only excited, but then creativity, invention, and discovery were flourishing.

> **Instead of one task, I offered a variety. All of a sudden, students who rarely handed in work, were actually into the assignments.**

Teacher as lecturer only.

Colleagues who refused to change from a totally lecture format of delivering information and having students take notes used the argument, "It was good enough for me; it builds discipline and makes them learn the information."

In fact, some older colleagues would snicker in the faculty room about any classes that were rumored to be "fun." They felt real learning could not possibly be going on in those rooms. I learned relatively quickly in my career those particular principles can be very lonely company when facing bored students day in and day out. We all know that it is hugely laborious to fight an uphill battle, and adolescents will make it doubly difficult with all of the fighter stealth they can muster. I am happy to say that a huge positive in education today is that teachers truly want student to enjoy their classes, are willing to be mentored, and are open to new ways of doing things.

Technology and accountability.

New teachers would often complain that though they were savvy about using technology, their adolescent charges were not always enthusiastic. They would create what they deemed "cool lessons and assignments" but still had huge accountability issues with students not following through! Middle school students who see their teacher day after day on a Smart Board without much interaction from "the gallery" might as well listen to a lecturer at a podium.

I welcomed technology in my classroom from the document camera to the Smart Board to podcasting. I had my own website on which I posted classroom news and assignments. I often took my students to the computer lab to produce their work and worked closely with the librarian on 21st century research methods.

Technology is one tool in the toolkit.

I used technology as one tool in my large tool kit. What I knew about my students in the latter years of my career was that too much of a good thing became very stale. I used all the various tools of technology in my bag of tricks to vary instruction or to break up a class period into modules due to diminishing attention spans. In my own learning experience, I had come to despise sitting through PowerPoint presentations because the format was extremely laborious for many types of presentations. So

> **The rule of thumb was that for me to use the technology, it had to increase student interaction in the lesson.**

the rule of thumb was that for me to use the technology, it had to increase student interaction in the lesson. Some examples of using technology in this way are instantly publishing student work on a document camera, analyzing and discussing a streamed-in film clip, or listening to a podcast and then debating the issue it raised. I always tried to embed alternate format choices for projects and assignments so that students could showcase the technology they enjoyed using.

Make students masters of their own learning.
Yet the closer I got to retirement, I felt that many of the school's technological investments were becoming "has beens" for middle school students whose primary relationship with technology was texting and plugging in to the outside world. But we can only do our best while these students are in our midst; by making them the masters of their own learning, we can yield results. If students are allowed to collaborate, motivation increases. If students are given choice, their inner spirit is often brought to the surface. If they are engaged in project-based learning, opportunities for self- directed inquiry, ingenuity, and critical thinking are built in.

As facilitators, we provide the framework for learning. Yes, we attend to the demanded skills of our assessments, the standards set forth by our states, and the initiatives of our employers. However, when the paradigm shifts just a bit, the facilitator reaps some rewards as well. Sitting and working alongside my students, I would share ideas and suggestions with them. Perhaps, the greatest benefit of all? I learned from them and was overwhelmed by the ideas, insights, and innovations that would flow freely in my classroom.

This did not happen simply because I wished it to be so. My secret was to fill that blank canvas not only with good, solid lessons, but with products of my imagination, my life experiences, enriching background information from many sources, relevant film and printed material—variety, variety, variety, detail, detail detail—and always with attention to what I had learned that middle school students need. The fruits of all that labor? My students were rarely bored, and neither was I.

8

A Balancing Act

My middle school students would always say that I have a passion for irony: from the ironies of real life to the great irony of an O. Henry story. There is nothing more ironic than attending to the classroom needs of adolescents—teachers constantly walk the high wire of balancing middle schoolers' need for structure and their need for variety.

Structure.
On the one hand, adolescents crave structure and guidelines and feel safe in the hands of an organized teacher. Students need to know why they "have to know this," and they need a great deal of hand-holding in terms of directions and outlined expectations. They need to know the "rules of the game" in everything that goes on from cooperative learning to test taking procedures to class presentations to grading criteria. I learned through the years that you get what you ask for: students require clearly explained requirements and expectations in their assignments.

> **You get what you ask for: students require clearly explained requirements and expectations in their assignments.**

Students also appreciate classrooms that run like well-oiled machines: folders in their proper baskets ready to be passed out by them, books neatly ordered on shelves ready to be distributed by them, and missed homework and project assignment sheets displayed in one place and ready for pickup by them. Middle school students love to be part of the day-to-day operation, you see.

Variety.
However, if you are too structured and never change things up, students will use their favorite six-letter word, "BORING!" The secret is that it's all a balancing act. Although this isn't a book on tips and strategies, per se, I thought I would share some of the ways that I kept my classes and my teaching from becoming stale or losing their edge.

Never be too predictable was my #1 law. I wouldn't do Monday business every Monday or Friday business every single Friday. I would change it up all the time. You get a sixth sense for knowing the crowd mentality when students come into the room. Often, I would make snap decisions and change the format for what I would do in a class period. For example, many middle school teachers like their early classes because the students are quiet and calm. I chalk that up to the fact that the kids are still groggy or half asleep. Those same students on a delayed schedule due to weather or a flipped schedule, perhaps for testing, could be a whole new entity! Often those students were zany and rambunctious and would require a different approach to the lesson.

Consider that bogeyman of all school children—dreaded Monday. If you ever heard the sixties rock group the Mamas and the Papas, you might remember a line they sang, "Monday, Monday, can't trust that day." That is never more true than at the middle level. For example, middle school students often come in on Monday whooping and hollering and wanting to chit chat with friends after a long weekend. They might need the pacifier of a short film clip to get them calmer and a bit more receptive to a serious discussion. Or conversely, on rainy Monday mornings I felt as though my students were the "walking dead," so a quick collaborative task may have been the way to go with students reporting out their findings. If we had been writing for long stretches of time, then I'd have them "publish" their work on the document camera. If they were struggling with poetry, I'd sit right down among them and write one of my own. For some strange reason, at least at my school, I found that Tuesdays and most Wednesdays were optimal instructional days. A corollary to my law, though, is that too much of anything, even if it is a good thing, becomes stale to middle school students.

Pique their interest was another law of mine, and I always gauged the success of my class by how it would have held my interest for forty-odd minutes. I became known for "being quotable." I adore quotations, and I stimulated their curiosity by putting on the board a Quote of the Week compatible with the themes of our learning for that particular week. I also quoted my favorite television shows. I am a *Seinfeld* fanatic, and one of my classic quotes was "Serenity now!" It helped lower my blood pressure, believe me, and caught on with my students, who started imitating me.

They also responded positively to my "inventions" of key words and phrases—especially the gently teasing names for them. For some reason I got away with calling my kids "happy hooligans" for 27 years. Other days I referred to them as "my chickadees" or when I was not happy with behaviors, "weisenheimers." To achieve quiet, I was known to say, "Quiet on the set!" or "Duct tape please; metaphorically speaking, of course!" or "Sorry to interrupt your social lives!" I also devised a system I referred to as "TG-13." As a Language Arts teacher, sometimes films and literature, as well as classroom discussion, could border on the inappropriate in terms of language or content, so I would use TG-13 as my middle school way of tempering the shock value and explaining the necessary realism. TG-13 translates to mean "teacher is in charge here, and there are very good reasons why we are talking about this maturely." If students saw my comfort level holding its own, they handled all types of controversial words, issues, and topics comfortably as well.

> If students saw my comfort level holding its own, they handled all types of controversial words, issues, and topics comfortably as well.

Change colors, another of my guiding principles, was inspired by chameleons. Just as chameleons signal their intentions by changing colors, I would do the same. Normally I am an even-keeled kind of person, but if I found that students were forgetting their manners or classroom etiquette, they would get a dose of tough love. If students were feeling "senioritis" after spring break heading toward the end of the school year, and other teachers were loosening up a bit, I would pump things up, not down. If I felt test preparation was stifling my students, I would bring in children's books for analysis or do some read-alouds which my students adored. I would also change the colors of the work I gave them to do. "Beware the five-paragraph essay" became one of my mantras. While this time-honored form of writing certainly had its place in my repertoire, I had students write responses in the form of letters, memos, critiques, and editorials. I found that I could get so much out of a short response and could do it with incredible frequency and give feedback sooner. The worn out end-of-term research paper became a magazine they published on a topic they wanted to pursue in-depth. Many times I had students draw or sketch their ideas, and graphic organizers in all shapes, sizes, and cool art forms entertained the students, but told me volumes about their learning.

Predictability, status quo, and lack of variety are not ingredients for success in the classroom. The secret was always about achieving balance—my positive energy, the students' positive energy, and the environment's positive energy—kind of my own brand of feng shui in the classroom.

9

Student Voice

Those of us in middle level education know the basics of adolescent psychology. Teens are naturally rebellious. Their state of mind isn't in a "state" at all; they are out-of-sync, their bodies out of control. They are asserting independence one minute, clinging for dear life to childhood the next. They can be moody, argumentative, and downright annoying. Over the years, many colleagues, especially younger teachers, after having observed my class as they walked by would ask me how I seemed to have such "control," such "order." They would comment about how engaged the students always seemed in my classroom. The secret, really, is that I learned early on that I would rather open the airways and purposefully hear the voices of my students rather than hear them talking or socializing in spite of my presence in front of the room. I also noted that many of the teachers who had students acting out were dogmatic, gavel-pounding types who insisted on their particular brand of "sameness." Because students did not have much of a voice in those classrooms, they found their own ways, often inappropriately, of being heard. So, I realized finding avenues for student voice would have to become part of my classroom practice.

> I would rather open the airways and purposefully hear the voices of my students rather than hear them talking or socializing in spite of my presence in front of the room.

Finding life lessons in the drama.
In middle school very often you have one of two choices when students charge into the classroom brimming over with the gory details of the latest

drama or arguing some real-life moral dilemma that has just reared its head. You can try to squelch it and proceed with your lesson. Good luck with that. Or you can allow your students to vent, which I heartily recommend. As you become adept at reeling in the conversation, with time you may even capitalize on the life lesson at the center of every good middle school controversy. The diehards among us say, "But the lesson is sacred." No lesson is being taught when the voices of students are louder than the moving lips in front of the classroom. The only one listening then is you — if you can hear yourself!

"Structured venting."

Venting sessions, an impromptu way of letting students be heard, can be structured in many ways. Whenever I planned a lesson, an activity, or a project, the bulleted checklist in my head always had a bullet for student voice. *Student voice* does not refer to answering teachers' questions. It means all the possibilities for student input that were natural extensions of what I was doing. If an assignment was due, instead of immediately collecting the papers, I would ask students to share them first. They might read their creative pieces aloud, summarize their research findings, or voice their opinions on the class novel they had just read. And, in later years I thanked the writing gods for the invention of the document camera, which enables instant publishing that allows students to see each other's products.

Student voice in assessment.

I came to solicit student input in assessment as a matter of course. When designing projects, I usually created a rubric to assess student work. Helping me define the various levels of the rubrics and the wording that accompanied each descriptor gave students a sense of ownership in the process while they internalized the grading criteria. Students would practice using the rubrics by grading some of my former students' projects, which I had saved with their permission. When I created essay and constructed response questions to assess learning, I used critical thinking questions suggested by students along with questions of my own. Seeing

> **Helping me create rubrics gave students a sense of ownership in the process while they internalized the grading criteria.**

them published along with teacher-made questions gave them a real sense of validation. When major project and assignments were due, I would solicit student input on what they considered fair penalties for late work. This definitely raised awareness, and it always amazed me how much tougher their penalties could be compared to those I was considering!

Student voice in group work.

Group work is another wonderful avenue for students to be heard. The collaborative approach naturally gives rise to student voice because they are engaged in discussion while completing a task. Obviously, I would want the class to hear what each group had learned, but it took me a while to refine the reporting out so that the class could distinguish how the various groups differed in reaching their outcomes. The longer I taught, the more I focused on having students examine their own learning, whatever the topic. I would ask students to report out on such things as

> **The longer I taught, the more I focused on having students examine their own learning, whatever the topic.**

- the substance of their discussion

- what led them to draw their conclusions

- what new ideas were gleaned from working with one another

- what questions were still unanswered

As educators, we tend to zero in on "the right answer," and miss so many opportunities to hear from kids about the dynamics of discovery which is central, I think, to all that happens in the middle school classroom.

Students as teachers.

I also used students as teachers whenever possible. For example, listening and note-taking are important skills in eighth grade, and often I would have students show the class their notes and explain in "student terms" what their note-taking strategies involved. After giving an assignment, I would ask students who felt comfortable with the directions to take the lead in explaining them to the class. If we were involved in a long-range project such as research, at different calendar points I would have students show what they accomplished, share the organizational approach that brought them to that point, and explain some of the difficulties they had and how they overcame them.

What those teachers who passed my room saw as "student engagement" was really a snapshot view of my classroom vision. As I evolved in the profession, I came to believe that a middle school classroom meeting the needs of adolescents should be a community of learners. On many days I had to be the focal point of instruction, but wherever, whenever possible, students were asked not only to be accountable for doing work and meeting deadlines, but also to be contributing voices. Often when an administrator or colleague walked into my class, they would have to find me among the sea of faces, because invariably students were at the helm. The secret, though, is that I was always the facilitator, creating opportunities for these "student teaching" experiences and guiding the students in these roles.

> **I would capitalize on every natural opportunity to allow student voice to substitute for my own.**

10

Pick Your Battles

If you become an educator, there is a huge chance that you have lofty goals and high ideals. Becoming a teacher is hard work in terms of the amount of course work required, and the practical experience of field work and observations is extremely time-consuming. It is an arduous journey to certification, and we do it because we want to make a difference in the lives of others. We have the best interests of students in mind, and that informs all that we do for them. We have firm belief systems about what is acceptable in terms of their academics, behaviors, and social interactions. Armed with my strong sense of ethics and values, as a new teacher I believed I could handle any situation involving my students. That vision quickly evaporated as adolescents enacted various moral dilemmas for my arbitration, ran amok with tons of infringements ranging from mild to serious, and tested the larger system by bending or out-and-out defying the student handbook rules. I remember the very first time I butted heads with a student, held my moral ground while chastising this student, and then felt completely miserable. While I don't remember the details of the infraction, to this day I do remember how awful I felt in the aftermath. When that happens frequently in the early years, a great deal of mental replaying of events, soul searching, and vital sleep loss usually leads to a shift in idealism.

If you are a control freak like me, then you may embrace the "them or me" view of things. I often said to myself, "Hey, I am the teacher, they are the students; therefore, my word is law!" What I learned through the years is that as the master of your ship you have to make adjustments for winds, currents, and rocky patches. In middle school, it comes down to ideals vs sanity. Adolescents are notorious for testing any system, so it is a given that they will do so in your classroom. The secret to dealing with this actually lies in what does *not* work. I have found that no amount of yelling, talking over students, embarrassing a student in front of others, or punishing the whole class for the sins of one (or a few) ever works for the long term. Neither does hypocrisy. Middle school teachers must self-assess for all the behaviors they find abhorrent in their students. In essence, do they break their own rules?

> **No amount of yelling, talking over students, embarrassing a student in front of others, or punishing the whole class for the sins of one (or a few) ever works for the long term.**

Handling your own problems.

There is something else at play that compromises our ideals, and I am not referring to the students themselves. Young teachers have a hard time coming to terms with this, but it is a reality nevertheless. I am talking about the administrators of the particular building in which you teach. I believe there is an invisible sign over most principals' and assistant principals' offices that reads something like this: "Take care of your own discipline problems! I have too much on my plate." I became familiar with this unwritten rule early on. Because I wrote very few referrals, I was a sweetheart with administration. When I did send occasional students to the office, they would report that they got the following speech: "Mrs. Scott never sends students to see me, so I know this is a very serious offense." I figured out for myself that teachers who sent kids to the office for the slightest infraction were looked upon unfavorably. I had to solve my own problems.

I think many teachers believe that their administrators should support them at every turn and are unpleasantly surprised when they don't. I agree with them in theory, but it just doesn't play out that way. Also, the trend over the last decade has been to have teachers call students' homes and come up with their own behavior intervention plans, making the last option going to the office. In fairness to all those administrators, they do have much on their plates, and I would not want their jobs. So we truly do have to fend for ourselves. Of course, there are the no-brainers of discipline that must be reported: violence, cutting class, and gross insubordination are just a few that come to mind. Teachers must be vigilant about complying with major school policies such as rules about electronics and mandates on bullying, so that students receive a consistent message about and enforcement of school rules.

Everyday nuisances.
But what about the microcosm of our own classrooms? How do we deal with the everyday nuisances, the constant adolescent behaviors that can drive us to distraction? Can we really write referrals for breaking pencils or passing gas? Maybe you are chuckling at this point, but the range of behaviors from slightly irksome to downright obnoxious can plague a middle school teacher and sap us of our much-needed energy. Here is just a smattering of what I could expect to encounter during any given day at the middle school besides the aforementioned destruction of writing implements or noxious flatulation: interrupting out of nowhere to go to the nurse, bathroom, or locker; eating snacks, texting, getting up to sharpen a pencil while I or another student was talking when no pencil was needed; doing/copying homework for another class; writing profanity or drawing body parts on desks; honking loudly while blowing nose; applying makeup or asking another student to fix one's hair.

As the years went on, my tolerance level grew, not diminished, for what I began to chalk up to typical middle school buffoonery. At the beginning of the year, I would outline my pet peeves and would include all the middle school nonsense of my former students. Along with getting a few "cheap" laughs, I got a lot of mileage out of putting it out there right away. But there are plenty of middle school students who love attention no matter how it is achieved, and I soon realized that their silly or over-the-top antics were inevitable. A good percentage of these behaviors I simply ignored, especially if I was the only one being derailed by the behavior and no turmoil ensued. Another good percentage I reacted to with humor, especially the burping and nose blowing; often a dramatic pause was sufficient, and then I'd move on. To the make-up appliers I would quip, "What is this—cosmetology class? Are you in the wrong room?" Usually they would shyly put their wares into their bags and get back to the business at hand. In the case of the gas passer, I would often admonish the rest of the class for reacting with guffaws and upturned noses by saying, "Pardon him—he's got a problem! What's yours?" Graffiti artists were met with my arsenal of desk cleaner, sponge, and paper towels; nothing needed to be said.

Interruptions.

Interruptions are button pressers for me. So, I would talk with students who interrupted when none of their peers were around. In many cases what worked like a charm was to say, "I know you would never intentionally hurt other people." Usually, the student would look at me shocked and aghast, and I would say, "Do you have any idea how hurtful it is to interrupt class when there are students who won't get the lesson as easily as you do because they got sidetracked?" Occasionally, a student would need a few gentle reminders, but for the most part, up close and personal quick discussions always yielded better results than yelling and screaming, especially in front of an audience.

Emails home.

If troublesome behaviors could not be channeled into an etiquette lecture, humorous moment, or one-on-one, sometimes a quick email home would be the way to go. I loved the advent of emails because parents would be able to think about the issues without getting defensive about their child as they tended to do on the phone. Most times they were mortified by such ridiculous or outlandish behavior and took care of the situation. If your school has teams and you encounter a problem not serious enough to call in a parent, you can use a method my team successfully used. We met as a team of teachers and called in the student in question. Many times just having to face an inquisition was enough to "scare the student straight!"

My intent is not to imply that teachers should overlook behaviors that interfere with instruction or defy what they feel are fair rules consistently applied. I am trying to say that the middle school classroom can, quite frankly, be a bizarre place where bad manners, clowning, and mischief can get the upper hand. Rather than have a steady stream of students head from your class to the main office, you must find ways to quell the "young and the restless."

First line of defense.

Laying it out there for students the first week of school was always my first line of defense, not in a dogmatic, preachy way but by explaining why those behaviors simply had no place in my classroom. I would share with kids that I worked very hard to make my class interesting and enjoyable, that my former students found my class to be a positive experience and would not *want* to misbehave. I also had my classes write letters to the incoming 8th graders outlining what to expect and how to "survive" Mrs. Scott's 8th grade English class.

> **I was never afraid to admit defeat to myself, but would go back to the drawing board to change lessons, change how I was reacting to my students, or contact parents.**

The new 8th graders loved those letters, my former students did all the work in setting them straight, and it set a great tone.

Second line of defense.

Having a variety of well-paced activities built into each class period was my second line of defense, and I was never afraid to abort or change midstream anything I felt was not going well. But I did it calmly, seamlessly, in control the whole time. Finally, I reflected all the time: period by period, after school, in the evening. I was never afraid to admit defeat to myself, but would go back to the drawing board to change lessons, change how I was reacting to my students, contact parents not so much with an SOS plea but to lay out concerns. And the beauty of teaching is that we get new clients every year. We have an opportunity to do some pretty heavy duty soul-searching over the summer and return steadfast and determined to put in place what we learned from our mistakes.

I think the secret to middle school discipline is to talk to kids. They are very reasonable beings when the teacher is not yelling, singling out, backing to the wall, playing favorites, or being inconsistent. You cannot have it both ways. You cannot be doing all those things then expect your students to consistently behave. I found that a calm demeanor, even if I was eaten up on the inside, was the answer.

> **I think the secret to middle school discipline is to talk to kids.**

Maintaining my cool at all times was the defuser for the petty nonsense that is the bane of all middle school teachers all the way up to those turbulent events that no teacher ever escapes completely.

11

Challenges

We have all heard people remark, "Kids today!" with a slightly curled lip and a shake of the head. In their searches for identity, teens have always had a notorious reputation for their rebelliousness, egocentrism, and outspoken nature. Every generation of teens has had its crazy music, outlandish fads, and its issues for protest, and today's teens are no exception. However, from an educational viewpoint, I will say that in my thirty years of relating to teens, I saw a gradual, but huge, change in them. Yes, adolescents have always presented teachers with unique challenges, but the numbers of students presenting challenges increased noticeably as my career progressed. There have always been struggling students, misbehaving students, unaccountable students, troubled students, but the sheer numbers of them have skyrocketed.

> **There have always been struggling students, misbehaving students, unaccountable students, troubled students, but the sheer numbers of them have skyrocketed.**

It is this volume of "hurting buckaroos" as I have been known to call them that frustrates and harangues the most patient, compassionate middle school teacher. It's important for those in the field to remind themselves why there are so many changes in today's students and that many of their concerns and frustrations are beyond their spheres of influence. Middle school teachers want to save every child, but, unfortunately, the baggage that some of their students carry to school each day prevents that from happening.

Increase in missing work.

Now mind you, all of my observations are nonscientific; they are simply noted trends and patterns as I sought reasons for my increased communication to students' parents, the need to track down students in study halls to make up work, or the constant heads-up to the guidance counselors that some students were not succeeding. At the beginning of my career, I always had a few students blow off the books I assigned or not hand in work on the due date. Very gradually, though, those numbers rose (especially the numbers of boys) with the advent of the more complex "toys" that consumed their energy. First, it was the dirt bikes and ATVs or quads, and then came the obsession of a large percentage of my students—the skateboard.

The freedom of "the ride" occupied many of my students for hours and hours, and the lure of the fields and trails was much stronger than the lure of meeting deadlines and getting homework done. My skateboarders were spending their time honing their skills and learning new and better tricks; they were completely and totally hooked. During this time the majority of my female students were still completing homework and observing deadlines.

Students' ability to focus.

I then began to notice ever so slightly a change in students' ability to focus. I had always had my share of daydreamers and doodlers, but this was more pronounced. Even the most reliable students seemed to be afflicted with a mild attention deficit issue. A possible explanation hit me when I attended the baby shower for my first grandchild. As I examined all the toys piled up and watched my new granddaughter play with them, I noticed every toy was ablaze with flashing colored lights, a cacophony of sounds, and multi-functions built into the object. Though I am no neuroscientist, I could not help thinking that these toys were wiring a different brain! Then when computers, cell phones, and the like hit the market, I noticed that all my students were beginning to rearrange their priorities, and school for many of them was not at the top of the list. Teachers started verbalizing their concerns: "These kids expect to be entertained!" "They don't want to read or write anymore!" and "Students know two words: *boring* and *fun*."

In the past few years, I have seen teachers throw up their hands. In spite of their best efforts to make class interesting and fun for their students, including the integration of technology, the accountability piece is at an all-time low. Many teachers feel they are working harder than ever before, their students less. Despite their best efforts, teachers are seeing many students underachieve or even fail. They plead for more guidance counselors, social workers, and school psychologists because a handful of a student's teachers just cannot do all that needs to be done to help that student succeed.

Use of non-school time.

Schools do not have steel walls impervious to the ailments that plague society. Middle school teachers spend an average of forty-five minutes, five days a week with their students. While their students optimally are engaged, enthused, and working hard during that time, the rest of their time is out of their teachers' control. When you stop to consider what the average adolescent is doing outside of school, you realize what teachers are up against. I noticed over the last few years how tired and ill-prepared my students were because they were admittedly on computers, playing video games, and texting into the wee hours of the morning. Students were also losing their innocence to the world of reality shows and to increasingly graphic and violent movies. They were losing the ability to be truly inspired because "they had seen it all." Many teachers will tell you that they have seen the boundary lines between student and teacher blurring over time. Some students attempt to talk to teachers as equals, severely compromising the respect factor.

Family issues.

The biggest detriment to student success, though, has been the change on the home front. With divorce rates, single parenting, and guardianship on the increase, I began to notice at parent/teacher conferences that I never knew who would show up: parents, step-parents, a boyfriend of the mother, a girlfriend of the father, grandparents with custody, guardians. Although it is very much a positive to have family members or guardians wanting to be involved, it is a big task to keep all the various people involved and following through. I also noticed a huge increase in absenteeism over the past few years. Many students are allowed to stay home for a variety of reasons besides illness including babysitting for siblings, sleeping in, or just chilling. These were all reported to me by my students themselves. But worst of all, when I think of how many abused, troubled, frightened students go to school each day, how can any of us expect that school is a high priority?

Value changes in society.
When I look at society at large, I often shake my head in frustration and sometimes downright disgust at a world gone haywire. Why shouldn't our students try to test the system, act out, or be apathetic when the adults in their midst no longer adhere to the simplest agreements upon which society used to be based: civility, rule following, strength of character? Driving, shopping, being in an audience, and dining out remind me that we have a serious shortage of role models.

Never give up.
With all that said, the one clear message every one of my students got was that I would never give up. I would not let them cop out because over and over, I would repeat, "Your education is everything!" With all the obstacles in the way, I would still communicate home (whatever that came to mean), track down students for work within their school day if I could not count on their after-school hours, and refer them to the appropriate support staff to help with their various needs. I came to realize that we have to do the best we can while our students are with us. My secret of success with my students was they knew I would never let up— they meant that much to me.

> **My secret of success with my students was they knew I would never let up—they meant that much to me.**

Changes for the better.
Yes, kids today really have changed…and in some ways, for the better. My students over time proved to be real risk takers: inventive and willing to tackle challenges. With each passing year they were capable of the most amazing insights, drawing parallels between school content and real-life application. Their sense of humor and irony always kept me on my toes.

And though they were outspoken in protest to perceived injustices, they were always quick to complement their fellow students and the teacher for a job well done. I felt students had increased empathy and tolerance especially in light of all the violence that was prevalent when I first started teaching middle school. I saw less shyness and more willingness to be part of a group as well as active participants in the classroom community. Students became more willing to share their gifts and talents. Creative energy, intuitiveness, dynamism, curiosity—I felt these increase over the years, and I really capitalized on those factors in planning lessons and projects. I believe these were wonderful outcomes of increased professional development over the years: cooperative learning, literature circles, authentic assessment, and reading/writing workshop. And though I was not always happy with the media my students were exposed to, I did feel my students were more aware of the world around them and less insulated. This made them more curious, looking for answers to some pretty critical questions, and much more energized and excited about issues.

Business model.

Whether we like it or not as educators, we have to deal with things not being the way they were in the past. Yes, kids absolutely have changed, and like it or not, the pressure is on *us* to find interventions, other avenues of instruction, our whole bag of tricks, if you will, to adapt to those changes. We are not miracle workers, and we will not save every child, but those of us in the middle know that we are in the greatest position to make a difference. Over the last decade I felt I had to redefine my role following the business world model. Successful business leaders will tell you that you have to create an environment where good things happen, where each individual feels visible and validated, and a part of the team. I provided that safe, collegial space for my students where individual thought, experience, and background were celebrated and encouraged. My students have told me that they felt my classroom was a place where they could bring the best of themselves, and in the ever-changing climate of my school, that was the very best I could ask for.

12

The Elephant in the Room: High Stakes Testing

I debated whether or not to go down the road of high stakes testing in this book because truly I could write a treatise on how much harm I believe it does. When I think of some of the great successes I have had with children over the years, those successes had very little to do with test results, performance growth indicators, or value-added models. Over the last decade I watched "the test" go from an instrument used to evaluate programs to one used to identify students in need of remediation. Then over the past few years, I watched it morph into the monster it has become. I can rant and rave about the costs to taxpayers, the socioeconomic bias of the tests, the valuable time that is eaten up by the administration and scoring of these tests, but truly, my bottom line is that these tests do not bear the slightest resemblance to what I did with students day to day, unit to unit, project to project. I think it is a gross injustice to students to reduce their progress and abilities to the outcome of a three-day test that is often loaded with ambiguous questions and questionable scoring procedures. But as all teachers must, once given the mandate, I climbed aboard "the testing train" and felt I owed it to my students to have them feel comfortable with test content and test procedures.

> **The great successes I have had with children over the years had very little to do with test results, performance growth indicators, or value-added models.**

The priority of testing.

What was most difficult for me was to give testing a prominent place among classroom priorities when I embraced it so un-wholeheartedly! But I felt

I could never let the kids down; therefore, I gave the speeches about the importance of testing and the importance of doing one's best, and slotted in practice tests along the way. As the testing movement gained even more momentum, especially in using student scores as a teacher accountability piece, the pressure on teachers was becoming more and more palpable in my school, and I, too, almost felt I had to transfer that pressure to my students. However, being the self-reflector that I am, I knew this was not right for my students and certainly not true to who I am. I had another of my moments of clarity and gradually put the bogeyman in his place.

Sacrificing time to test prep.
I always believed that the middle school classroom was the laboratory for students to experiment, satisfy their curiosity, and discover the world and themselves. I believed that the majority of work assigned should be authentic and inquiry-based. I felt students' writing folders should be a compilation of all types of writing from narratives, to analyses, to critiques, to research, as well as the constructed response, the main written component of our state assessments. I especially wanted them to write about themselves, a most important exercise for adolescents who get to know themselves through journal writing and self-analysis. I wanted them to read tons of adolescent fiction in which they could explore in-depth themes relevant to their lives. I wanted them to read and perform plays, write and analyze poetry, and savor short story and nonfiction pieces beyond the "surface" requirements of an assessment. I wanted to devote the meager time I was allotted each day to these pursuits, not sacrifice precious minutes to test prep. I stayed true to those beliefs despite the increase in testing mania.

Embed the assessment skills.
I studied the assessments in depth and worked extremely hard to embed the demanded skills of the assessments into my own rich curriculum. I used great works of literature and nonfiction rather than photocopied former tests and designed questions and writing tasks that went way beyond the scope of the test. I tapped the students' critical thinking at every turn with quotations, moral dilemmas, newspaper and magazine clippings, and Internet tidbits that posed universal questions and conflicts. We read, we wrote, we

discussed. And in my efforts to have students examine their own learning and take charge of it, I had them dissect those photocopied tests. I had them rip apart questions to determine their purpose and the skills required to answer them. I had them read passages and design better questions than the ones on the test. I had them formulate their own extended response questions to pieces that they read and then answer them.

Yes, "the test" would continue to cast its shadow, and yes, I still did some practice tests and gave tips and strategies on how to ace the test because I wanted my students comfortable and in control on those test-taking days. As a school community, we sensed the foreboding as test days approached on the calendar, and faculty meetings were devoted to the coming assessments. The "test" continued to be a presence in my classroom, but now in its proper place, as we went about our other business.

Speak candidly to students.

Once again, as in so many legs of my middle school journey, the secret was I had to find a happy medium when I was at odds with the system. What it always came down to was that I had to do right by my students first, then myself. I dealt with the whole testing scene the same way I dealt with many sticky situations in education: I spoke candidly to my students about it. I explained that state assessments were a component of my professional obligations just as they were a component of their academic lives, and I would use my knowledge of the test and my expertise to help them succeed. I got them on board by explaining my methods of embedding skills, and I would point them out along the way relating them back to the test. I had them examine their own learning and watched them become much more engaged because they were analyzing those photocopied packets rather than merely filling them in.

My students never felt they were drilled to death, but they did feel they could meet assessment challenges head on. Here again was another irony: the specter of testing that had reached crisis proportions in my own mind led to a whole new course of action that benefited my students in the end, sort of an educational "lemons to lemonade" story, if you will.

13

Parents—Allies or Enemies?

Sounds ominous, doesn't it? Truthfully, the majority of parents and guardians I have encountered over the years have been supportive, wanting what is in the best interest of their children, my students. They came to open houses, parent-teacher conferences, they responded to calls and emails and worked hard to keep their adolescents on the straight and narrow. They were appreciative of all the hard work teachers put forth and expressed their gratitude for doing a job they knew was not easy. The majority of parents were my greatest cheerleaders, thanking me for the job I was doing with their children, spreading the word to other parents, and requesting me for their other children.

Reaching out to parents.
Through the years I responded in kind in a few different ways. I tried to make my open houses interesting and informative, worth their efforts for coming out in the evening after a tiring day of work. For example, just the way I wrote poems for my students, I wrote poems for parents and guardians— they got a huge kick out of that. It was a great opener, and then I would explain my course outline or the state tests their children faced. Just as I mixed it up for students, I did the same for their parents. I often sent notes home complimenting good behavior and effort when I saw it, rather than always sending home negative news. When parent-teacher conferences were scheduled,

> I wanted parents and guardians to feel we were in it together, not adversaries on opposite sides of the table.

I prepared. I had work samples, current averages, comments on strengths and areas in need of improvement. I tried to remember how daunting it is to sit across from the person who sees a whole other side of your child. In a word, I was welcoming. I wanted parents and guardians to feel we were in it together, not adversaries on opposite sides of the table.

That said, there has been a growing trend over the years to challenge the old notion of "the teacher is the parent in absentia; the teacher's word is law." Many of my older colleagues and I remember the days when teachers had God status and woe to the child if a parent was ever contacted about misbehavior or missing work. Much has changed in the parent/teacher relationship, and it comes down to parent expectations about what that entails. There is more of a defensive posture between the parties whether the discussion is a child's behavior, a child's accountability, a parent challenge of classroom practices, curriculum, or teacher communication.

Accountability.

Most of the time parents really want to work with the teacher to end behaviors that are impediments to learning—their child's and the rest of the classes'. I did meet parents, though, through the years who fell into categories I had created in my head. The toughest category to deal with was the "not my child" group. These parents were often in denial which usually led to the blame game: the teacher, school, or other kids must be at fault. The secret to dealing with these folks was to garner as much information from other teachers as possible or have a team meeting with the child's teachers and the parents—not to gang up on them, but to present a united front in wanting the best for the student and a quick resolution. The same went for accountability. It would be important to know where a student was falling through the cracks with assignments and preparedness so that all teachers and the parents could follow through by signing off on a homework planner. The key to success was all parties following through, but often the system would break down. The teachers I worked with tried to be so diligent about planners or calendars only to be thwarted by the lack of parent monitoring. In fact, I categorized many parents as those who never followed through. We could meet, communicate, and put the child on a weekly planner. I'd feel we were on the same page, but nothing changed because the parents did not hold up their end of the bargain.

Communication with parents.
While I was often frustrated with the "in denial parents" who would make up endless excuses rather than face the truth, there was another category of parents that made me see red: the parents who ignored progress reports, report cards, emails, and calls, and then surfaced at the end of the school year when so much damage had already been done. In my calmer moments, though, I would remind myself that parenting is the toughest job, and parenting an adolescent is the toughest job of all. In my heart of hearts I knew that, and I gave parents as many chances as I gave my students. In fact, one of the most time-consuming parts of my job was parent communication—about behavior to some extent, but mostly about work owed. Often my friends and family would wonder what lesson I was teaching students by going after the work and constantly getting parents involved—how was that teaching

> One of the most time-consuming parts of my job was parent communication—about behavior to some extent, but mostly about work owed.

responsibility? Believe me; I pondered that question many times over the years. The bottom line for me was that work owed is work not done. Work not done means lack of practice and lost skill. It is so easy to give out zeroes, but I wanted my students to follow through. And as new teachers learn very quickly, administrators zero in on teachers who have too many students failing their courses.

Parents *are* watching.
For the most part, I had the respect and cooperation of most of my parents through the years, so it was very difficult for me when the occasional parent would put me on the defensive. Until the day I retired that was not a place in which I ever felt comfortable—feeling attacked or violated. I learned over the years that parents *are* watching, and I think that is a good thing. But teachers will tell you that parents can overstep the boundaries, calling teachers on everything, from taking something that was said in class out of context on the authority of their child or the child's friends, challenging an assignment

or grade by going to the principal rather than discussing it with the teacher first, making accusations or threats without any preliminary discussion with the teacher. Many teachers today feel vulnerable and open to attack. My worst feelings of violation, though, came from parents who challenged the materials I used. I had parents who objected to some class novels and stories for religious reasons or personal philosophy, and though I always had the support of my principals and my school district, I felt violated. I could defend every book based on its literary merit, every story for its universal themes, but that never made it any easier to have what I perceived as my professional judgment called into question.

Helicopter parents.
New teachers going into the field are often broadsided by the scope of parent control today. And the administrators of any school, but definitely, at the middle level, will tell you that the majority of their day is spent dealing with parents. Every school has its share of "helicopter parents" as they are called. Their presence in the school is well known. They head to the principal's office with a list of grievances, often engineer their children's schedules in the guidance office, and seem to have a presence in every office in the school. Although our ideals as public school teachers dictate a certain egalitarian approach to all parties in the school community, somehow, with these parents, something beyond tact and diplomacy is necessary—political savvy, if you will. Although it seems blasphemous to play such games, the reality is that administrators often set the stage for these parents, giving them wide berth to air grievances or allowing them special privileges they might not otherwise confer. You learn who these parents are, and you learn to play politics.

Over time I learned the secret to effectively engaging with parents is the same used in dealing with their children: tact, diplomacy, and patience. In my beginning years of teaching I would get very frustrated and stressed out by parental challenges. Later on it became second nature, like any acquired skill, to remain calm and respectful, hear the parent out, acknowledge the difficulty of parenting an adolescent, and work toward solutions. This is part of the job, like it or not, and with practice, parents, for the most part, will be a teacher's allies—not the enemy!

14

Surviving the Stress

If all that hat wearing, role playing, and performing seem as though they might just be exhausting, BINGO!!! They are. No way is teaching middle school for weaklings. I am not talking about needing muscle strength; I am referring to mental agility, emotional and intestinal fortitude, and tons of true grit that are required to hang out with adolescents all day. Of course, all jobs today coupled with 21st century busy schedules equate to a population that is, by and large, exhausted most of the time.

> Teaching middle school zaps your strength, because of all the mental gymnastics necessary to do the job well.

However, teaching middle school zaps your strength, I think, because of all the mental gymnastics necessary to do the job well.

Let's face it. Handling adolescents is difficult for their own parents. Parents will tell you it's a chess game of strategy to get through the day: the hormones; the rebellion; the know-it-all syndrome; the attitudes and chips-on-the-shoulder; the neediness one minute, aloofness the next. Now, our job as teachers is to get along with these kids; impart instruction that may not necessarily interest them; listen to their complaints and confessions; answer tons of their questions, some unanswerable; and be the "center of eyes" for long stretches of time. As a teacher, you are always on. You can't shut the door to the office and zone out or blow off steam. You can't run to the lavatory and throw cold water on your face. It's you and them.

The need for stamina.

It doesn't matter what your age is. I've talked to brand new teachers who say they are totally wiped out; they never expected middle school to be so draining. Young, middle-aged, or heading toward retirement, you need to be on top of your game, and you need tons of energy. When folks hear that you teach middle school, reactions are often mixed. Some give you their blessings with a sorrowful shake of the head. Others say, "They couldn't pay me enough!" The message is clear: not everyone can do the job of a middle school teacher. I think what others are really saying is they don't have the stamina and energy to deal with the likes of adolescents. What always amazed me most was that the results of a restful, re-energizing summer could vanish within the first few weeks of starting a new school year!

Mastering tact.

The hard work and preparation tend to be the easy part of being a middle school teacher. For me, the most fatiguing part of the job was mustering the tact that I think is the key secret to success in teaching adolescents. They are a fragile bunch; they bruise and even break so easily. A smiling face can become a mask of doom in seconds. So many students needed a kid-glove approach, and I tend to be a shoot-from-the-hip kind of person. So while my dry sarcasm worked on a small segment of my student population, I found that unless I wanted to retrace my steps with some kids and do damage control, I had to develop the mental acuity to deal with each and every one of them as individuals. I had to know what pushed their buttons, what level of humor they responded to, how much constructive criticism they could tolerate, read their body language, and infer between the lines of what they said. This level of analysis applied to over 100 students would wipe anybody out!

> **The most fatiguing part of the job was mustering the tact that I think is the key secret to success in teaching adolescents.**

Constant decision making.

Add to the "tact factor" the decision-making process. In our private lives we make many decisions, some of them tough and leading to much angst. As teachers, we are constantly bombarded with decision-making dilemmas coming from so many different angles: central administration, the principal, the guidance office, our respective subject area departments, parents, and even our colleagues. But when you teach adolescents, their very nature springs decisions at you at every turn. Should you put the lesson aside to deal with a dilemma that has presented itself? Should you extend that homework assignment because sports and other activities have some students under pressure? Should you address the student in the back writing a note? Should you

> **I had to develop the mental acuity to deal with each and every one of them as individuals.**

pretend you didn't hear the whispered foul language? Should you persevere even though the student in front of you is picking his/her nose? Should you rip up/take away the math homework being done while you are teaching? Should you investigate whether or not that student is texting in his pocket? (Yes, it is done all the time!) Should you grimace at the stench emanating from one student's proud expulsion of gas or just go on? Should you wake up Sleeping Beauty who was probably up all night playing video games? And these are the easy ones! Should you? Should you? Should you? This is the key question multiple times a period, every period, every day.

Take care of yourself.

So what is the secret to finding limitless amounts of energy, tact, and resilience in making the big decisions required at the middle school level? Healthy living! You need to eat well, sleep well, and take care of your health. You need to come to school each day recharged, motivated, and ready-to-go. It is so hard to fake it if you have been up all night or missed meals or didn't do whatever it takes in your life to recharge your battery. For me, it was always about getting up earlier than I needed to in order to meditate over that first cup of coffee and evolve into the Energizer Bunny as I am known to some. It was about getting to school earlier than most so I could evolve into my role. And though often washed out at the end of the day, I always tried to exercise to walk off my stress or revel in the day's successes. Sometimes I would hit the rail trail, run an errand, or sit in the car and listen to music for a few extra minutes because there is no doubt in my mind that middle school teachers need a little space in between dealing with their students and the people in their private lives.

You cannot cope with the roller coaster ride that is middle school if your reserves are almost on empty. It's not really important how you get your groove on; it is just important that you do. But I can tell you, the mental and emotional calisthenics are much more tolerable when you are rested, upbeat, and in control. In fact, I chuckle at the contrast between my drive to work in the morning and my return home. In the morning I would be pumping up the volume of my favorite rock station to get psyched and energized for a day at the middle school. However, on my ride home, I would have to listen to classical music to still myself, lower my blood pressure, and find some inner peace so I could face phase two—my other life!

Other antidotes.

I have heard many antidotes to middle school madness over the years. Many teachers enjoy a nice glass of wine or two in the evening, but I found that would only make me grumpy in the morning, so that was not a workable solution for me. I had to come in full of energy and verve, not drag myself in. I know many teachers who herald Wednesdays as over-the-hump day, and pray for the coming of Fridays and the next holiday break. On the other hand, I am a proponent of a carpe diem philosophy and refused to wish my life away, so that would not do. I know many educators who leave what happens in school at school; they have an uncanny ability to leave their problems behind, forget about everything, and come back to face another day. Again, not a solution for me. I was always someone who took the job home with me, physically in terms of papers and reading, but also mentally, replaying scenes from the day, going over and over and over and over (no exaggeration) something I might have said that had been taken the wrong way, the questionable way I handled a certain situation, or, perhaps a really bad decision I had made. And yes, no matter how excellent a teacher you are, no matter how preemptive you are, no matter how well-loved you are, you will beat yourself up on many occasions on all sorts of things from classroom blunders such as sarcasm with a bit too much of a razor's edge aimed at a student to wider school community snafus like an email that probably never should have been sent.

My system.

Little by little, I realized I had invented my own system of dealing with unpredictable, over-the-top, annoying, frustrating, sometimes outrageous adolescents, as well as parents, and yes, at times, colleagues and administrators. I was labeled a "quiet listener" in meetings, so "calm and collected" in dealing with students, and "the voice of reason" in dealing with my peers. Meanwhile, inside my head, simultaneously, I might be calling these people every name in the book or sending them over a cliff or using brute force or duct taping their mouths in a mental film clip. I started calling these imaginings "the bubbles in my head," a thousand different cartoon strips of the brain that kept me out of so much hot water. I even started using this technique outside of school, but that's a whole other book.

How my system works.

The beauty of my system was that it gave me a place to immediately react to what I was feeling without opening my mouth and possibly regretting anything I might say or do. I would then be able to take a deep breath and be a bit more staid in my reaction. In fact, often negative feelings would just pass, and I would be able to move on. That is actually a lesson I learned from my students. One of the secrets of dealing with adolescents is that now and again you learn terrific things from them. Middle school kids can be very forgiving and move on pretty easily. I could be agonizing about some issue with a particular student or students that had them in the pits of despair, and while I was still consumed, they had already moved on. That may not be so for the parents who get wind of teacher error, so my Number One rule for myself was, "When in doubt, don't say it!" My best policy if I was questioning myself was to wait and consider my next course of action rather than regret an in-the-moment reaction.

Failing that…

If my "bubble system" failed, there was always one other tactic that usually restored my sanity when all else failed. I went shopping! I called it my weekend "M & M." I felt I was entitled to a little treat when I had survived working another week at what I dubbed "the hooligan hotel"! I don't mean to give the impression that middle schools are so zany that teachers have to resort to the extremes of wine, wishing their lives away, or going into credit card debt. In fact, the environment can be relatively calm and businesslike. But usually when it got like that, my radar would tell me that a storm could very well be brewing. Perceptive middle school teachers know that the next drama is usually lurking right around the corner.

15

Who Made a Difference?

You hear it all the time. "The rewards of teaching." "Teaching is such a rewarding experience." Mere hollow words. And how could I possibly talk about rewards when I have recounted the exhaustion, the head games, the frustrations, the tears, the battles, the compromises that were the sum total of my career? Add to that the never-ending hard work. These hooligans, nudges, and wisenheimers (said only with love, laughter, and a gleam in my eye) often had crying spells and dramatic outbursts, as well as bouts of forgetfulness; they were guilty of rude interruptions, insensitive remarks, and chronic self-absorption. Middle school students quite simply can be among the moodiest, most irksome of all creatures. But if you can reach them, really delve into their hearts and minds, the return on your emotional investment is like nothing you have ever experienced! It is a payback of such intensity that I become bleary eyed at the very thought of it.

When middle school students love you, they are euphoric about it. They shower you with compliments, write poems and notes, and draw pictures for you. They look you in the eye and tell you how wonderful you are. They bring you little gifts, and they hang around after class so they can chat. When a middle school child decides you are worthy of their love and respect, there are no barriers like there may be between you and other loved ones.

Love spills over into learning.
But the true payoff is what happens with all that positive energy. The love spills over into the learning, and you may hear your students say, "I love

this class," or "I wish I could stay here all day," or "We learn so much here," or "You taught me things I never, ever thought about before." You hear parents say, "My daughter talks about you all the time!" or "My son comes home every day and tells us about the stories you read," or "I hope my other children will get to experience your class." You have former students come back to visit or write to you, and your heart swells because they still remember works they read, projects they worked on, or how much they loved being in your classroom.

When my career ended, I walked away with almost thirty years' worth of fulfillment and an enormous sense of accomplishment. There were the honors and accolades from colleagues and administration. I received a rousing send off, and I am still receiving congratulations from parents and former students. Speeches were made on my behalf; notes, cards, and letters were written. The consensus is that I was perceived as passionate, dedicated, and hardworking, and had made a difference in my students' lives. But is that really how it went down? Was it I who made the difference?

The theme that keeps playing in my mind is the difference that they made in my life. The students, the parents, the school community all contributed to my learning, my growth. Yes, on the face of it, sometimes they challenged me, were demanding, and put up obstacles in my path. Sometimes they stretched me to the max, made me dig deep, and sent me back to the drawing board. I became more self-aware. What I felt sometimes as "going against my principles" was really opening myself up to new ways of looking at things, developing more empathy, trying to see the other side of issues instead of only my side. I learned my capacity for hard, challenging work. I discovered the actor, counselor, mediator, referee, and fashion consultant in myself. I uncovered and used my gift of writing in so many beneficial ways. I learned that I had to take care of my physical and emotional health, so I could be at the top of my game. I learned the art of diplomacy, the number one skill necessary to navigate the world of middle school and still

> **What I felt sometimes as "going against my principles" was really opening myself up to new ways of looking at things, developing more empathy, trying to see the other side of issues.**

keep my head on straight. I had to grow with the times, especially using technology, considering I began teaching in the days when mimeograph machines were the vogue. I found that my own painful adolescence was reborn as my happier inner child working at the middle school level, and the serious, unhappy eldest child of an alcoholic had a lighthearted, humorous corner of her heart set free by hanging around adolescents.

> **I learned the art of diplomacy, the number one skill necessary to navigate the world of middle school.**

As I scan the years, I am able to see how an educational philosophy evolved. What does any kid out of college know about what is truly right for kids? The first time you enter a classroom, it is with a fairly simplistic recipe in hand: usually a generous helping of teaching the way you were taught; some tidbits you picked up in your educational course work, student teaching, and field work; and your ideals. It is baptism by fire, and you hope for the best.

It was my students who would come to inform all that I now believe about their education—not the well-intentioned colleague down the hall, not the mandates coming down from State Ed, not even the convictions I had about what constitutes a good education. It was my students who were aching to be inspired; it was my students wanting constant feedback so they could grow and improve; it was my students who wanted variety and engagement; it was my students who needed compassion, caring, and someone to listen to them; it was my students who completed projects and assignments when they were authentic, relevant, and meaningful. These students were not numbers on a state's sliding scale of competence. Developmentally and emotionally they were all over the map! Each was a living, breathing being with individual needs, certain strengths, and certain weaknesses, coming together into my classroom. Bound together in our relationship, not by choice for any of us when we started, we discovered new worlds, revealed secret parts of ourselves, discussed universal truths and the great questions; we worked, struggled, progressed and grew.

16

Students Have the Last Word

Adolescents are known for having to have the last word whether in an argument with parents or a scrap with a sibling. It is no different in school. Whether a student is angry with a friend, trying to be the center of attention in a class discussion, or engaged in verbal fisticuffs with a teacher, it is natural for a middle school student to end it all with "the last word." Despite the flourishes, drama, and fanfare that embellish adolescent diatribes and opinions, there is often a kernel of truth to what they say if adults are open enough to hear it. Adolescents are too easily dismissed as hormonal loonies who don't know what they are talking about. Some of the best advice, lessons, and words of wisdom I ever received came from my students through the years. And so it is fitting that I end with students and allow them the last words.

Student views.
My students would give their opinions on a range of topics, whether solicited or not. But one topic in which I was keenly interested throughout my career was the role of teacher from their point of view. I wanted to know how students knew good teaching when they saw it. I wanted to know what it took to earn their respect. I wanted to know what they felt was bad teaching and how a teacher could improve. I wanted to know what their education meant to them. I wanted to know what their best teachers had in common. Of course, I always wanted to know these things to monitor my own teaching. But I had many education students from local colleges come to observe my class, supervised countless student teachers, and also

mentored young teachers in my building. I wanted to pass on my students' views to them. In fact, when I had student teachers coming to work with me, I would hand them letters of advice from my students on "How to Succeed in Teaching."

Balance.

Though the names and faces of my students changed from year to year, their views on teaching were similar. Patterns began to emerge in their expectations of their teachers, changes they would like to see in certain classrooms, and what it takes to earn students' respect and cooperation. Now, of course, any adolescent who is given carte blanche wants candy, parties, movies, and no homework all under the auspices of a totally cool, fashionable young teacher! However, once you get past letting students design their middle school utopia, they are usually very sensible and responsible about stating their views. The one word that came up over and over in my discussions with students and in their writing about the topic of teaching was "balance." They believe the secret to successful teaching, if I may translate into my own words, is almost a yin and yang in teacher qualities, behaviors, and management that complement one another and come together in the classroom.

> **Students believe the secret to successful teaching is almost a yin and yang in teacher qualities, behaviors, and management.**

In my students' estimation, teachers have to have a sense of humor but need to know when to be serious. They have to be smart and knowledgeable about content but have to make it easy for their students to understand. They have to be interesting, passionate, and dynamic, but they must never be fake. They have to love kids, be compassionate and friendly, but they must never stand for nonsense. They have to be organized and disciplined, but they must be flexible. They have to have high standards but understand when students are having problems or cannot always meet deadlines. They should be creative and fun, but sometimes "go by the book." They have to be strict and in control, but know when to lighten up. These are not opposites, really, just all degrees in the fine art of balance.

The non-negotiables.

The majority of my students recognized that in teaching as in life there are always those non-negotiables like rules of safety, items in a curriculum that must be covered, and school district policies that must be enforced. Those non-negotiables exist for students as well. They believe that all teachers should love and be able to relate to kids or find another job, be non-judgmental and never play favorites, believe in their students, and above all, be fair and consistent.

Well, I said adolescents were tough! They want their teachers to be a master blend like a fine wine or an outstanding coffee with pronounced overtones but subtle nuances of this or that as well.

> All teachers should love and be able to relate to kids; be non-judgmental and never play favorites; believe in their students; and above all, be fair and consistent.

In talking to many students I had in the past, in fact sometimes children of former students I had who would become my students as well, I would hear a familiar refrain that became a truth about teaching. Though they would remember bits of the curriculum or some of the books they read in my class or were able to visualize the classroom they sat in day in and day out, it was "the person" they remembered most. They remembered inspiring moments, words of encouragement, a kind deed, a strong but loving lecture, helpful comments on a paper, a life lesson that stayed with them. They remembered the wit, the expressions, and the personal stories. And so they validate what I have come to believe is the key to teaching at the middle level, the secret to working with adolescents: **In order to teach them, you have to reach them.**

About Association for Middle Level Education

Since its inception in 1973, the **Association for Middle Level Education (AMLE)** has been a voice for those committed to meeting the educational and developmental needs of young adolescents. AMLE is the only national education association dedicated exclusively to the growth of middle grades education.

With more than 21,000 members representing principals, teachers, central office personnel, professors, college students, parents, community leaders, and educational consultants across the United States, Canada, and 46 other countries, AMLE welcomes and provides support to anyone interested in the health and education of young adolescents. In addition, AMLE has a network of 58 affiliate organizations in the United States, Canada, Europe, and Australia, strengthening our outreach to the regional, state, provincial, and local levels.

Through the release of our landmark position paper *This We Believe: Keys to Educating Young Adolescents*, AMLE has been a key resource to middle grades educators focused on developing more effective schools. Our message is for schools to be academically excellent, developmentally responsive, and socially equitable for every young adolescent.

AMLE publishes *AMLE Magazine, Middle School Journal*, and *Research in Middle Level Education Online* to support members throughout the year, in addition to publishing books on a wide variety of middle level education topics. Our website, www.amle.org, provides a wealth of research and resources for educators, a complete online bookstore, and professional development event information. In addition to our annual conference, one of the largest professional development events in education today with nearly 6,000 attendees, AMLE offers a wide variety of more specialized professional development opportunities, including customized on-site professional development.

For more information about AMLE and our services, visit www.amle.org or call 1.800.528.6672